# SCHOLASTIC

# Addition & Subtraction Practice Ages 5-7

**Revision & Practice**

**KS1 Years 1-2**

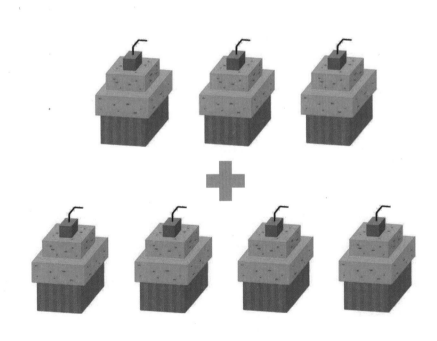

Build confidence with targeted skills practice

**SCHOLASTIC**

Published in the UK by Scholastic, 2024

Scholastic Distribution Centre, Bosworth Avenue, Tournament Fields, Warwick, CV34 6UQ

Scholastic Ireland, 89E Lagan Road, Dublin Industrial Estate, Glasnevin, Dublin, D I I HP5F

A catalogue record for this book is available from the British Library.

ISBN 978-0702-32685-1
Printed and bound by Ashford Colour Press

The book is made of materials from well-managed, FSC®-certified forests and other controlled sources.

MIX
Paper from responsible sources
FSC® C011748

**Author**

Paul Hollin

**Editorial team**

Rachel Morgan, Vicki Yates, Kate Baxter, Julia Roberts, David and Jackie Link

**Design team**

Dipa Mistry and Juliet Knight

**Illustrations**

Mario Gushike/Astound

# Contents

# How to Use this Book

## Introduction

This book has been written to help boost the addition and subtraction skills your child has been learning at school. It is designed to reinforce the core mathematical principles to develop knowledge and confidence, which will be invaluable as they progress.

Topic title

Each page starts with a **Recap** of relevant background knowledge your child should already know.

The key content for the area is covered in the **Learn** section. There are clear explanations and examples, using illustrations and diagrams where relevant.

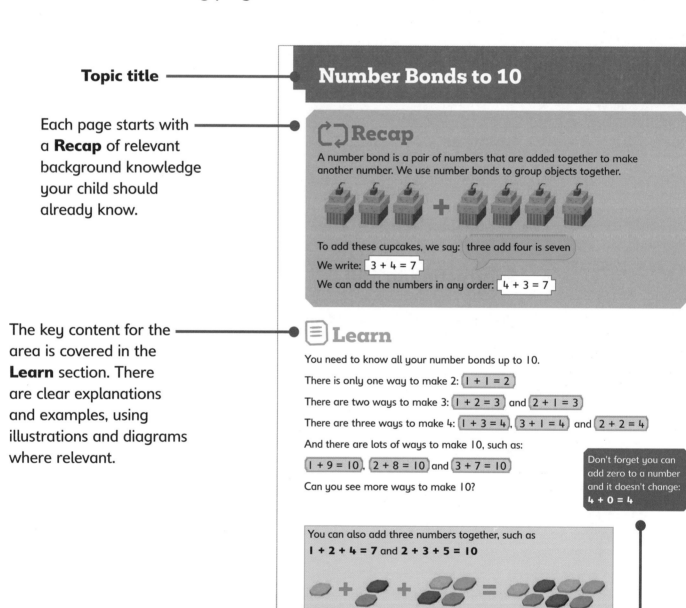

### Number Bonds to 10

#### ↻ Recap

A number bond is a pair of numbers that are added together to make another number. We use number bonds to group objects together.

To add these cupcakes, we say: three add four is seven

We write: $3 + 4 = 7$

We can add the numbers in any order: $4 + 3 = 7$

#### ▤ Learn

You need to know all your number bonds up to 10.

There is only one way to make 2: $1 + 1 = 2$

There are two ways to make 3: $1 + 2 = 3$ and $2 + 1 = 3$

There are three ways to make 4: $1 + 3 = 4$, $3 + 1 = 4$ and $2 + 2 = 4$

And there are lots of ways to make 10, such as:

$1 + 9 = 10$, $2 + 8 = 10$ and $3 + 7 = 10$

Can you see more ways to make 10?

Don't forget you can add zero to a number and it doesn't change: $4 + 0 = 4$

You can also add three numbers together, such as
$1 + 2 + 4 = 7$ and $2 + 3 + 5 = 10$

8

**Tips** provide short and simple advice to aid understanding.

**Practice** ●──────────────────────────────────────── **Practice** a focused range of questions, with answers at the back of the book. To check progress and give practice in what they've learned.

1. **Write the correct number bond for each picture.**

a.

b.

_____ + _____ = _____          _____ + _____ = _____

2. **Without using zero, write all the number bonds for each number.**
   The first two have been done for you.

| 2 | 1 + 1 |
| 3 | 1 + 2 and 2 + 1 |
| 4 | |
| 5 | |
| 6 | |
| 7 | |
| 8 | |
| 9 | |
| 10 | |

3. **Write the missing numbers.**

a. 3 + _____ = 5          b. 8 + 2 = _____          c. _____ + 4 = 10

d. 0 + _____ = 6          e. 1 + 3 + 4 = _____          f. 3 + 2 + _____ = 9

# Number Facts

 **Recap**

These ten digits make all our numbers:

| 0 | 1 | 2 | 3 | 4 | 5 | 6 | 7 | 8 | 9 |
|---|---|---|---|---|---|---|---|---|---|
| zero | one | two | three | four | five | six | seven | eight | nine |

There are 5 cubes in this row.

There are 8 ducks on the pond.

Numbers can be odd or even.

Even numbers end in 0, 2, 4, 6 or 8. They can be shared equally into two groups.

Odd numbers end in 1, 3, 5, 7 or 9. They can't be shared equally into two groups.

 **Learn**

We use the same digits to make bigger numbers. Look at the number fourteen. It has 1 ten and 4 ones. We write it 14.

| 10 | 11 | 12 | 13 | 14 |
|---|---|---|---|---|
| ten | eleven | twelve | thirteen | fourteen |

| 15 | 16 | 17 | 18 | 19 | 20 |
|---|---|---|---|---|---|
| fifteen | sixteen | seventeen | eighteen | nineteen | twenty |

We can describe and compare different numbers. Read these facts:

6 is **less than** 9

14 is **greater than** 11

**half of** 6 is 3

19 is **one more** than 18

**double** 7 is 14

15 is an **odd number**

12 is an **even number**

8 is **one less than** 9

# ✏️ Practice

**1.** **Write the number of objects in each picture. Circle even or odd.**

**a.**

☐ ducks    ( even ) or ( odd )

**b.**

☐ counters    ( even ) or ( odd )

**c.**

☐ people    ( even ) or ( odd )

**d.**

☐ cubes    ( even ) or ( odd )

**2.** **Write the missing numbers on these number lines.**

**a.**

0    1    2    ☐    4    5    6    7    ☐    9    10

**b.**

11    ☐    13    14    15    16    ☐    18    19    20

**3.** **Complete these statements using numbers or words.**

**a.** 6 is one more than _____

**b.** 13 is one less than _____

**c.** 16 is an _____ number

**d.** 9 is an _____ number

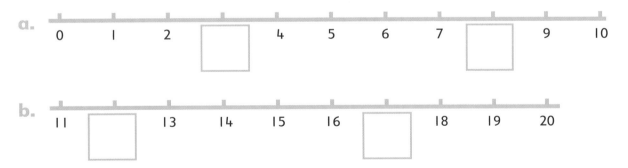

# Number Bonds to 10

## ⟳ Recap

A number bond is a pair of numbers that are added together to make another number. We use number bonds to group objects together.

To add these cupcakes, we say: three add four is seven

We write: $3 + 4 = 7$

We can add the numbers in any order: $4 + 3 = 7$

## 📄 Learn

You need to know all your number bonds up to 10.

There is only one way to make 2: $1 + 1 = 2$

There are two ways to make 3: $1 + 2 = 3$ and $2 + 1 = 3$

There are three ways to make 4: $1 + 3 = 4$, $3 + 1 = 4$ and $2 + 2 = 4$

And there are lots of ways to make 10, such as:

$1 + 9 = 10$, $2 + 8 = 10$ and $3 + 7 = 10$

Can you see more ways to make 10?

> Don't forget you can add zero to a number and it doesn't change: $4 + 0 = 4$

You can also add three numbers together, such as

$1 + 2 + 4 = 7$ and $2 + 3 + 5 = 10$

 **Practice**

**1.** Write the correct number bond for each picture.

a.

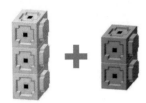

_____ + _____ = _____

b.

_____ + _____ = _____

**2.** Without using zero, write all the number bonds for each number.
The first two have been done for you.

| 2 | 1 + 1 |
|---|---|
| 4 | |
| 5 | |
| 6 | |
| 7 | |
| 8 | |
| 9 | |
| 10 | |

**3.** Write the missing numbers.

a. 3 + _____ = 5

b. 8 + 2 = _____

c. _____ + 4 = 10

d. 0 + _____ = 6

e. 1 + 3 + 4 = _____

f. 3 + 2 + _____ = 9

# Number Bonds to 20

## ↻ Recap

We can use a number line to help us write number bonds.

0  1  2  3  4  5  6  7  8  9  10  11  12  13  14  15  16  17  18  19  20

If we start at 9 and count on 2, we get 11. We write $9 + 2 = 11$

Some number bonds are doubles. We know that $5 + 5 = 10$

Use the number line to check these doubles:

$6 + 6 = 12$      $7 + 7 = 14$      $8 + 8 = 16$      $9 + 9 = 18$

## 📄 Learn

11 is one more than 10, so $5 + 6 = 11$ and, of course, $6 + 5 = 11$

We can use other bonds to make 11:  $1 + 10$   $2 + 9$   $3 + 8$   $4 + 7$   $5 + 6$

and we can reverse the order too:  $10 + 1$   $9 + 2$   $8 + 3$   $7 + 4$   $6 + 5$

- Bonds with 10 are the easiest to remember:
  $10 + 5 = 15$        $7 + 10 = 17$

- Use your bonds to 10 to help remember your bonds to 20:
  $3 + 5 = 8$, so $13 + 5 = 18$

- Use the 'one more, one less' rule:
  $10 + 4 = 14$, so $11 + 4 = 15$, and $9 + 4 = 13$

Be careful crossing 10, such as $8 + 3$. These are the harder bonds to learn.

The greater the number, the more number bonds it has. 20 has 21 number bonds!

 **Practice**

**1.** **Write all the number bonds for each number in the box next to it.**
One number bond has been done for you.

a. 12    | 1 + 11 |

b. 15    | 9 + 6 |

**2.** **Draw a line from each double to its answer.**

| 9 + 9 |    | 6 + 6 |    | 3 + 3 |    | 8 + 8 |

| 12 |    | 16 |    | 18 |    | 6 |

**3.** **Write the answers.**

a. 12 + 3 = _____        b. 14 + 5 = _____        c. 11 + 4 = _____

**4.** **Write the missing numbers.**

a. 4 + _____ = 12        b. 10 + _____ = 14        c. _____ + 2 = 11

**5.** **Try these three-number additions.**

a. 3 + 4 + 8 = _____        b. 7 + 0 + 3 = _____        c. 10 + 4 + 3 = _____

# Simple Subtraction

##  Recap

There are 5 birds in the tree, but 2 birds fly away. There are now 3 in the tree.

We can write [ 5 − 2 = 3 ]

0 1 2 3 4 5

We can say this in different ways.

> Five minus two equals three.

> Five take away two equals three.

> Five subtract two equals three.

##  Learn

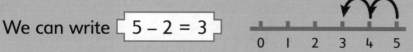

0 1 2 3 4 5 6 7 8 9 10 11 12 13 14 15 16 17 18 19 20

We can use the number line to help us subtract. We simply count back. Look at these subtractions and check them on the number line:

( 7 − 5 = 2 )  ( 14 − 7 = 7 )  ( 12 − 12 = 0 )  ( 19 − 4 = 15 )  ( 5 − 0 = 5 )

Can you see what happens if...

- You take away zero? ·········▶ The number stays the same.
- You take away a number from itself? ·····▶ The answer is zero.

To practise, choose any number above 10 on the number line and quickly say any subtractions that you are confident about.

> sixteen minus one is fifteen

> sixteen minus ten is six

> sixteen minus six is ten

> sixteen minus eight is eight

# Practice

**1.** **Draw these subtractions on the number lines.**

a.      b.

**2.** **Write and complete these calculations.**
The first one has been done for you.

a. Six take away two: __6 − 2 = 4__     b. Five minus four: _____

c. Twelve subtract eight: _____     d. Sixteen minus nine: _____

**3.** **Solve these subtractions.**

a. $16 - 6 =$ _____     b. $17 - 7 =$ _____     c. $18 - 8 =$ _____

d. $15 - 15 =$ _____     e. $15 - 0 =$ _____     f. $18 - 9 =$ _____

g. $16 - 8 =$ _____     h. $14 - 7 =$ _____     i. $12 - 6 =$ _____

**4.** **Write the missing numbers.**

a. $20 -$ _____ $= 10$     b. $20 -$ _____ $= 0$     c. $20 -$ _____ $= 13$

d. $20 -$ _____ $= 7$     e. _____ $- 8 = 10$     f. _____ $- 4 = 6$

g. _____ $- 3 = 7$     h. $13 -$ _____ $= 11$     i. _____ $- 12 = 7$

# Numbers to 100

## ↻ Recap

We use a base 10 number system.

10 ones make 1 ten                    10 tens make 1 hundred

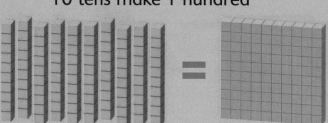

We can use digits to represent any quantity.

Here is 37.

3 tens          7 ones

## 📄 Learn

Here is a 100 square.

- Each **row** has ten numbers: 1 to 10, 11 to 20, 21 to 30. What comes next?

- In each **column**, the ones in the numbers are always the same. 3, 13, 23, 33. What comes next?

- If you're adding numbers together, find the number you need to start with and count on the number of squares you want to add. If you want to subtract numbers you count backwards.

- For **23 + 5**. You start at 23 and count on 5. The answer is 28.

Remembering your number bonds to 10 makes some calculations with bigger numbers easy.

47 − 4 = 43

| | | | | | column | | | | |
|---|---|---|---|---|---|---|---|---|---|
| 1 | 2 | 3 | 4 | 5 | 6 | 7 | 8 | 9 | 10 |
| 11 | 12 | 13 | 14 | 15 | 16 | 17 | 18 | 19 | 20 |
| 21 | 22 | 23 | 24 | 25 | 26 | 27 | 28 | 29 | 30 |
| 31 | 32 | 33 | 34 | 35 | 36 | 37 | 38 | 39 | 40 |
| 41 | 42 | 43 | 44 | 45 | 46 | 47 | 48 | 49 | 50 |
| 51 | 52 | 53 | 54 | 55 | 56 | 57 | 58 | 59 | 60 |
| 61 | 62 | 63 | 64 | 65 | 66 | 67 | 68 | 69 | 70 |
| 71 | 72 | 73 | 74 | 75 | 76 | 77 | 78 | 79 | 80 |
| 81 | 82 | 83 | 84 | 85 | 86 | 87 | 88 | 89 | 90 |
| 91 | 92 | 93 | 94 | 95 | 96 | 97 | 98 | 99 | 100 |

row

Notice how we just add or subtract the ones:
7 − 4 = 3, so 47 − 4 = 43

# Practice

**1. Write the number shown in each set of tens and ones.**

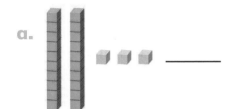

a. _____

b. _____

c. _____

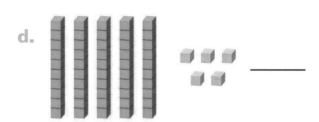

d. _____

**2. Use the 100 square below to help you solve these calculations. Shade each answer on the 100 square, then write the answer.**
The first one has been done for you.

a. 5 + 3 = __8__

b. 22 + 5 = _____

c. 83 + 7 = _____

d. 46 + 1 = _____

e. 15 – 4 = _____

f. 28 – 6 = _____

g. 99 – 10 = _____

h. 48 – 8 = _____

| 1 | 2 | 3 | 4 | 5 | 6 | 7 | 8 | 9 | 10 |
|---|---|---|---|---|---|---|---|---|----|
| 11 | 12 | 13 | 14 | 15 | 16 | 17 | 18 | 19 | 20 |
| 21 | 22 | 23 | 24 | 25 | 26 | 27 | 28 | 29 | 30 |
| 31 | 32 | 33 | 34 | 35 | 36 | 37 | 38 | 39 | 40 |
| 41 | 42 | 43 | 44 | 45 | 46 | 47 | 48 | 49 | 50 |
| 51 | 52 | 53 | 54 | 55 | 56 | 57 | 58 | 59 | 60 |
| 61 | 62 | 63 | 64 | 65 | 66 | 67 | 68 | 69 | 70 |
| 71 | 72 | 73 | 74 | 75 | 76 | 77 | 78 | 79 | 80 |
| 81 | 82 | 83 | 84 | 85 | 86 | 87 | 88 | 89 | 90 |
| 91 | 92 | 93 | 94 | 95 | 96 | 97 | 98 | 99 | 100 |

# Inverses

## Recap

It is important to learn number bonds. The more we practise these, the more we learn the patterns, and the faster we become.
Read each of these aloud. Do you understand them?

$6 + 5 = 11$    $5 + 6 = 11$      $2 + 8 = 10$    $3 + 7 = 10$    $4 + 6 = 10$

$10 + 7 = 17$    $10 + 8 = 18$    $10 + 9 = 19$

## Learn

When you understand the connection between addition and subtraction, calculations become easier.

Look at these calculations. Do you notice anything?

$4 + 5 = 9$        $9 - 4 = 5$

They show that addition and subtraction are inverses. This means they use the same numbers but in a different order.

Look at these four calculations. They all use the same numbers, but for two different operations.

$11 + 5 = 16$        $5 + 11 = 16$

$16 - 11 = 5$        $16 - 5 = 11$

If we start with one number bond, we can write two inverse calculations.

Look at these calculations and their inverses.

$5 + 3 = 8$            $7 + 4 = 11$            $20 - 8 = 12$

$8 - 5 = 3$    $8 - 3 = 5$        $11 - 7 = 4$    $11 - 4 = 7$        $12 + 8 = 20$    $8 + 12 = 20$

 **Practice**

**1. Draw lines from each addition to both of its subtraction inverses.**
One has been done for you.

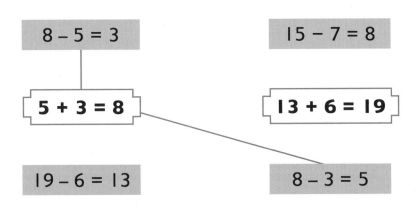

| 8 – 5 = 3 | 15 – 7 = 8 | 19 – 13 = 6 |

| 5 + 3 = 8 | 13 + 6 = 19 | 8 + 7 = 15 |

| 19 – 6 = 13 | 8 – 3 = 5 | 15 – 8 = 7 |

**2. Write the three related calculations for each of these number bonds.**
One has been done for you.

a. 3 + 2 = 5     $\underline{2 + 3 = 5}$     $\underline{5 - 3 = 2}$     $\underline{5 - 2 = 3}$

b. 6 + 3 = 9     _____     _____     _____

c. 12 + 3 = 15     _____     _____     _____

**3. Write the four calculations you can make with each set of numbers.**
One has been done for you.

a. 1, 2, 3     $\underline{2 + 1 = 3}$     $\underline{1 + 2 = 3}$     $\underline{3 - 2 = 1}$     $\underline{3 - 1 = 2}$

b. 4, 7, 11     _____     _____     _____     _____

c. 5, 14, 19     _____     _____

_____     _____

d. 10, 18, 28     _____     _____

_____     _____

# Bridging and Partitioning

## ↻ Recap

Knowing your number bonds to 20 helps you to add and subtract quickly.
If you need some more practice have another look at page 10.

## 📄 Learn

Number bonds, and addition and subtraction, are a bit harder when we have to cross a multiple of 10.

$$8 + 5 = 13 \qquad 14 - 8 = 6 \qquad 16 + 5 = 21 \qquad 21 - 4 = 17$$

Bridging can help make it easier. Let's try $47 + 8$

We know that $8 = 3 + 5$

So, we can say that $47 + 3 = 50$ and then add 5 to get $50 + 5 = 55$

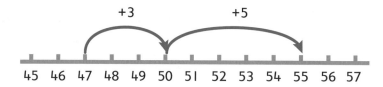

So $47 + 8 = 55$

We can use bridging to subtract too. This number line shows that $83 - 7 = 76$

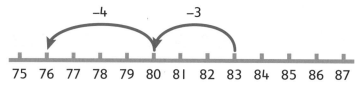

When we add and subtract larger numbers, partitioning can help.

We split, or partition, each number into tens and ones.

Add the tens together, then add the ones together.

**32 + 25**

30 + 2    20 + 5

**50 + 7 = 57**

Partitioning works for subtraction too, but you must be careful.

 **Practice**

1. **Draw on the number lines to use bridging, then write the answers.**
   One has been done for you.

   a.
   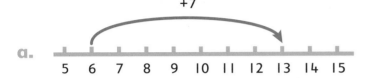
   +7

   5  6  7  8  9  10  11  12  13  14  15

   6 + 7 = __13__

   b.

   15  16  17  18  19  20  21  22  23  24  25

   18 + 5 = _____

   c.

   25  26  27  28  29  30  31  32  33  34  35

   33 − 5 = _____

   d.

   85  86  87  88  89  90  91  92  93  94  95

   94 − 9 = _____

2. **Use partitioning to add and subtract these larger numbers.**
   One has been done for you.

   a. 23 + 12:  __20__ + __10__ = __30__ and __3__ + __2__ = __5__

   so __30__ + __5__ = __35__

   b. 21 + 25: _____ + _____ = _____ and _____ + _____ = _____

   so _____ + _____ = _____

   c. 78 − 47: _____ − _____ = _____ and _____ − _____ = _____

   so _____ + _____ = _____

 **Recap**

Knowing your number bonds to 20 is important, especially when you cross over a multiple of 10.

For example, if you haven't learned 8 + 5 by heart, remember that you can

split the 5 and say $\boxed{8 + 2 = 10}$ then $\boxed{10 + 3 = 13}$

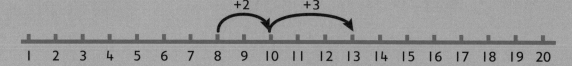

 **Learn**

We can understand addition using tens and ones equipment.

This shows $\boxed{35 + 22}$

Look carefully. There are **5** tens and **7** ones.

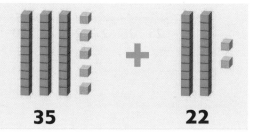

Or, we could do this with a number line.

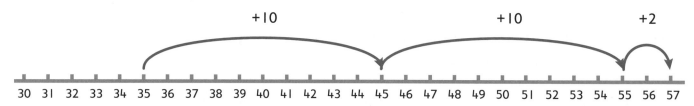

Look at this calculation: $\boxed{48 + 15}$

Adding the tens is easy. We have 4 tens and 1 ten, which is 5 tens.

But the ones are tricky. 8 ones plus 5 ones is 13 ones, or we can say 1 ten and 3 ones.

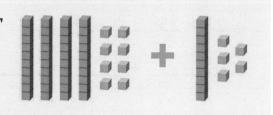

We have 6 tens and 3 ones altogether, so $\boxed{48 + 15 = 63}$

 # Practice

**1. Solve these additions using equipment.**

a.

a. _____ + _____ = _____

b. _____ + _____ = _____

**2. Solve these additions using number lines.**

a. 16 + 13 = _____

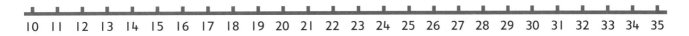
10 11 12 13 14 15 16 17 18 19 20 21 22 23 24 25 26 27 28 29 30 31 32 33 34 35

b. 11 + 23 = _____

10 11 12 13 14 15 16 17 18 19 20 21 22 23 24 25 26 27 28 29 30 31 32 33 34 35

c. 79 + 18 = _____

75 76 77 78 79 80 81 82 83 84 85 86 87 88 89 90 91 92 93 94 95 96 97 98 99 100

**3. Write the missing numbers in the spaces below.**

a. 18 + 4 = _____    b. 78 + 4 = _____    c. 69 + 15 = _____

d. 46 + _____ = 57    e. 66 + _____ = 90    f. 35 + _____ = 81

##  Recap

Subtracting is the inverse of adding.

If $7 + 6 = 13$ , then we also know that $13 - 6 = 7$ and $13 - 7 = 6$ .

Look at the number lines.

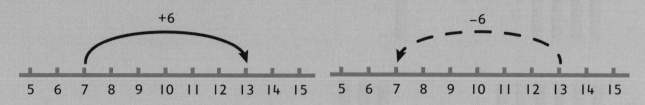

##  Learn

We can understand subtraction using tens and ones equipment.

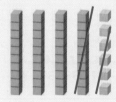

Can you see how to subtract 15 from 46?

15 is 1 ten and 5 ones. Take them away and we have 3 tens and 1 one left. Can you check it?

$46 - 15 = 31$

Subtraction gets harder when we have to cross a multiple of 10. Let's try $24 - 8$

We can easily take away 4 ones, but we need to take away 4 more.

The next 4 comes out of one of the tens. So, $24 - 8 = 16$

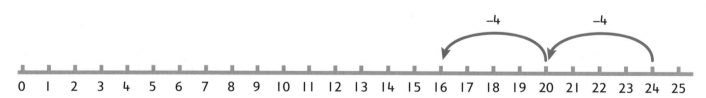

Can you see what $24 - 20$ will be?

We just take away the 2 tens and we have

4 ones left: $24 - 20 = 4$

# Practice

**1.** **Use the pictures to help you answer these subtractions.**

a. 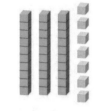    $37 - 6 =$ _____

b. 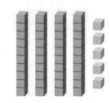    $45 - 8 =$ _____

c. 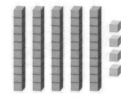    $54 - 16 =$ _____

**2.** **Solve these subtractions using number lines.**

a. $25 - 10 =$ _____

| 10 | 11 | 12 | 13 | 14 | 15 | 16 | 17 | 18 | 19 | 20 | 21 | 22 | 23 | 24 | 25 | 26 | 27 | 28 | 29 | 30 |

b. $36 - 13 =$ _____

| 20 | 21 | 22 | 23 | 24 | 25 | 26 | 27 | 28 | 29 | 30 | 31 | 32 | 33 | 34 | 35 | 36 | 37 | 38 | 39 | 40 |

c. $90 - 24 =$ _____

| 65 | 66 | 67 | 68 | 69 | 70 | 71 | 72 | 73 | 74 | 75 | 76 | 77 | 78 | 79 | 80 | 81 | 82 | 83 | 84 | 85 | 86 | 87 | 88 | 89 | 90 |

**3.** **Write the missing numbers in the spaces below.**

a. $13 - 4 =$ _____    b. $25 - 7 =$ _____    c. $90 - 15 =$ _____

d. $25 -$ _____ $= 20$    e. $33 -$ _____ $= 20$    f. $71 -$ _____ $= 69$

# Solving Problems: Money

## ⟳ Recap

We use pounds and pence for money.

There are 100 pence (p) in £1.

There are six coins that are worth less than £1.

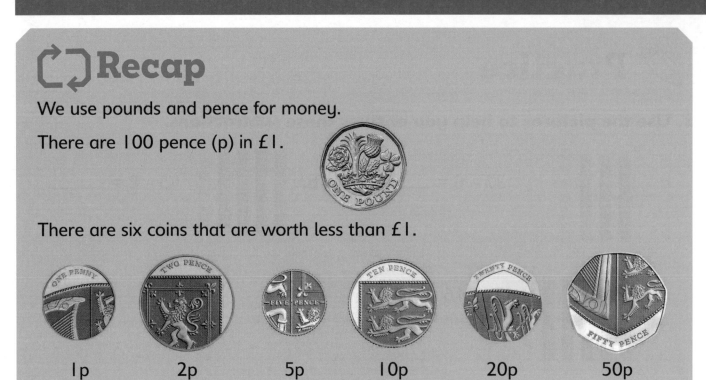

| 1p | 2p | 5p | 10p | 20p | 50p |

## 📄 Learn

Using money is a great way to practise adding and subtracting up to 100.

50p + 20p = 70p

55p + 12p = 67p

£1 − 56p = 44p

65p − 43p = 22p

 **Practice**

**1. Write and solve the calculation for each set of coins.**

a. 20p  +  10p  2p          _____ + _____ = _____

b. 50p  5p  +  20p 1p 1p    _____ + _____ = _____

c. £1  −  10p 10p 10p        _____ − _____ = _____

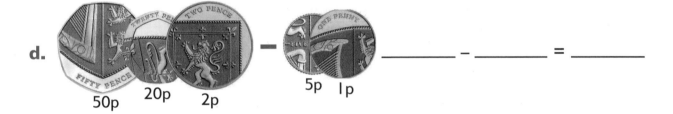

d. 50p 20p 2p  −  5p 1p      _____ − _____ = _____

**2. Solve these calculations.**

a. 25p + 11p = _____      b. 14p + 66p = _____      c. 37p + 28p = _____

d. 40p − 11p = _____      e. £1 − 26p = _____       f. 85p − 8p = _____

**3. Solve these problems.**

a. Ted has 33p and his gran gives him 48p.
How much money does he have now?          _____

b. Joni has £1. She buys a pen for 50p,
and a pencil for 13p.
How much money does she have left over?    _____

# Solving Problems: Measures

##  Recap

It's really useful to practise your maths in practical ways.
Remember: We measure lengths in centimetres.

We measure mass in grams.

We measure capacity in millilitres.

##  Learn

When adding, make sure the quantities you are adding have the same units and always show the units in your answers.

→ 8cm        → 5cm

Two pencils are 8cm and 5cm. What length are they if you put them together?

8cm + 5cm = 13cm

A jug has 80ml of water in it, but 25ml is spilled. How much water is left?

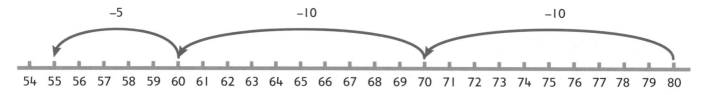

80ml – 25ml = 55ml

# Practice

## 1. Add these lengths.
One has been done for you.

pencil 1 — 7cm

pencil 2 — 5cm

pencil 3 — 6cm

**a.** pencil 1 + pencil 2: __7__ cm + __5__ cm = __12__ cm

**b.** pencil 2 + pencil 3: _____cm + _____cm = _____cm

**c.** pencil 3 + pencil 1: _____cm + _____cm = _____cm

## 2. Add or subtract these masses.

 rubber 56g

 pencil 23g

ruler 42g

 sharpener 31g

**a.** ruler + pencil: _____g + _____g = _____g

**b.** pencil + sharpener: _____g + _____g = _____g

**c.** rubber – ruler: _____g – _____g = _____g

## 3. Add or subtract these capacities.

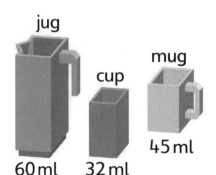

jug

mug

cup

60 ml    32 ml    45 ml

**a.** jug + cup = _____ml + _____ml = _____ml

**b.** cup + mug = _____ml + _____ml = _____ml

**c.** jug – mug = _____ml – _____ml = _____ml

## ↻ Recap

We can add and subtract numbers up to 100 using different methods to help us:

- ✓ Using a number system that has **tens and ones**.

- ✓ Knowing your **number bonds** to 10 and to 20.

- ✓ **Bridging** when crossing a multiple of ten.

- ✓ **Partitioning** to add and subtract bigger numbers.

- ✓ Knowing that addition and subtraction are **inverses** and so can be used to check each other.

## ✏ Practice

**1. Write the correct number bond for each picture.**

a. _____ + _____ = _____       b. _____ + _____ = _____

**2. Write the missing numbers.**

a. 2 + 2 + 5 = _____       b. 7 + 6 = _____       c. 3 + _____ = 11

d. 9 + 3 + 5 = _____       e. 19 – 9 = _____       f. 20 – 15 = _____

g. _____ – 6 = 10       h. 12 – _____ = 10       i. _____ – 2 = 17

**3.** **Draw on the number line to use bridging, then write the answer.**

0  1  2  3  4  5  6  7  8  9  10  11  12  13  14  15  16  17  18  19  20

8 + 5 = _____


**4.** **Use partitioning to subtract these larger numbers.**
One has been done for you.

a. 37 – 23:  __30__ – __20__ = __10__ and __7__ – __3__ = __4__

so __10__ + __4__ = __14__

b. 17 – 15: _____ – _____ = _____ and _____ – _____ = _____

so _____ + _____ = _____

c. 78 – 47: _____ – _____ = _____ and _____ – _____ = _____

so _____ + _____ = _____


**5.** **Solve these calculations.**

a. 4p + 5p + 3p = _____        b. 17p + 40p = _____

c. 93p – 23p = _____        d. 45cm + 10cm = _____

e. 67cm + 23cm = _____        f. 25g + 15g = _____

g. 42g – 16g = _____        h. 18ml – 11ml = _____

i. 98ml – 75ml = _____        j. 76ml – 37ml = _____

# Answers

## Pages 6–7 Number Facts

1. a. 3 odd   b. 8 even   c. 6 even   d. 13 odd

2. a. 3, 8   b. 12, 17

3. a. 5   b. 14   c. even   d. odd

## Pages 8–9 Number Bonds to 10

1. a. 3 + 2 = 5   b. 4 + 3 = 7

2. **4:** 1 + 3, 3 + 1, 2 + 2

   **5:** 1 + 4, 4 + 1, 2 + 3, 3 + 2

   **6:** 1 + 5, 5 + 1, 2 + 4, 4 + 2, 3 + 3

   **7:** 1 + 6, 6 + 1, 2 + 5, 5 + 2, 3 + 4, 4 + 3

   **8:** 1 + 7, 7 + 1, 2 + 6, 6 + 2, 3 + 5, 5 + 3, 4 + 4

   **9:** 1 + 8, 8 + 1, 2 + 7, 7 + 2, 3 + 6, 6 + 3, 4 + 5, 5 + 4

   **10:** 1 + 9, 9 + 1, 2 + 8, 8 + 2, 3 + 7, 7 + 3, 4 + 6, 6 + 4, 5 + 5

3. a. 2   b. 10   c. 6
   d. 6   e. 8   f. 4

## Pages 10–11 Number Bonds to 20

1. a. 1 + 11, 11 + 1, 2 + 10, 10 + 2, 3 + 9, 9 + 3, 4 + 8, 8 + 4, 5 + 7, 7 + 5, 6 + 6

   b. 1 + 14, 14 + 1, 2 + 13, 13 + 2, 3 + 12, 12 + 3, 4 + 11, 11 + 4, 5 + 10, 10 + 5, 6 + 9, 9 + 6, 7 + 8, 8 + 7

2.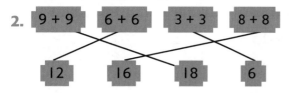

3. a. 15   b. 19   c. 15

4. a. 8   b. 4   c. 9

5. a. 15   b. 10   c. 17

## Pages 12–13 Simple Subtraction

1. a.            −4         b.            −3

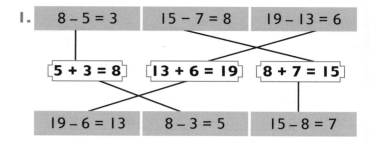

2. b. 5 − 4 = 1   c. 12 − 8 = 4   d. 16 − 9 = 7

3. a. 10   b. 10   c. 10   d. 0   e. 15
   f. 9   g. 8   h. 7   i. 6

4. a. 10   b. 20   c. 7   d. 13   e. 18
   f. 10   g. 10   h. 2   i. 19

## Page 14–15 Numbers to 100

1. a. 23   b. 36   c. 43   d. 55

2. b. 27   c. 90   d. 47   e. 11   f. 22
   g. 89   h. 40

## Pages 16–17 Inverses

1.

| 8 − 5 = 3 | 15 − 7 = 8 | 19 − 13 = 6 |

| **5 + 3 = 8** | **13 + 6 = 19** | **8 + 7 = 15** |

| 19 − 6 = 13 | 8 − 3 = 5 | 15 − 8 = 7 |

2. b. 3 + 6 = 9, 9 − 6 = 3, 9 − 3 = 6

   c. 3 + 12 = 15, 15 − 12 = 3, 15 − 3 = 12

3. b. 4 + 7 = 11, 7 + 4 = 11, 11 − 4 = 7, 11 − 7 = 4

   c. 5 + 14 = 19, 14 + 5 = 19, 19 − 14 = 5, 19 − 5 = 14

   d. 10 + 18 = 28, 18 + 10 = 28, 28 − 10 = 18, 28 − 18 = 10

## Pages 18–19 Bridging and Partitioning

1. b. 23　　c. 28　　d. 85

2. b. 21 + 25: 20 + 20 = 40 and 1 + 5 = 6
   so 40 + 6 = 46

   c. 78 – 47: 70 – 40 = 30 and 8 – 7 = 1
   so 30 + 1 = 31

## Pages 20–21 Adding to 100

1. a. 43 + 12 = 55　　b. 67 + 32 = 99

2. a. 29　　b. 34　　c. 97

3. a. 22　　b. 82　　c. 84　　d. 11
   e. 24　　f. 46

## Page 22–23 Subtracting to 100

1. a. 31　　b. 37　　c. 38

2. a. 15　　b. 23　　c. 66

3. a. 9　　b. 18　　c. 75　　d. 5
   e. 13　　f. 2

## Pages 24–25 Solving Problems: Money

1. a. 20p + 12p = 32p　　b. 55p + 22p = 77p
   c. £1 – 30p = 70p　　d. 72p – 6p = 66p

2. a. 36p　　b. 80p　　c. 65p　　d. 29p
   e. 74p　　f. 77p

3. a. 81p　　b. 37p

## Pages 26–27 Solving Problems: Measures

1. b. 5cm + 6cm = 11cm
   c. 6cm + 7cm = 13cm

2. a. 42g + 23g = 65g
   b. 23g + 31g = 54g
   c. 56g – 42g = 14g

3. a. 60ml + 32ml = 92ml
   b. 32ml + 45ml = 77ml
   c. 60ml – 45ml = 15ml

## Pages 28–29 Addition and Subtraction Practice

1. a. 2 + 1 = 3　　b. 7 + 2 = 9

2. a. 9　　b. 13　　c. 8　　d. 17　　e. 10
   f. 5　　g. 16　　h. 2　　i. 19

3. 13

4. b. 17 – 15: 10 – 10 = 0 and 7 – 5 = 2
   so 0 + 2 = 2
   c. 78 – 47: 70 – 40 = 30 and 8 – 7 = 1
   so 30 + 1 = 31

5. a. 12p　b. 57p　c. 70p　d. 55cm　e. 90cm
   f. 40g　g. 26g　h. 7ml　i. 23ml　j. 39ml

# Progress Tracker

*Well done!*

You have completed the
**Addition & Subtraction Practice** book

Name: _____

Date: _____